Quantum Attitude

Planning Your Business

Cyle Grieve

DEDICATION

To Sharri whose love gives me the strength to accomplish all I do, and to our two wonderful children Jamie Allyson and Benjamin Alexander. And finally to my lovely parents who have always supported me.

CONTENTS

ACKNOWLEDGMENTS

I would like to thank my friends and family along with those who have or are now serving their country. And all the people who strive to not only better themselves but those around them as well.

FORWARD

Most of us today have at one time or another been exposed to the phrase "The Law of Attraction". The Law of Attraction presumes that what you reap is what you sow. There have been many books, audio recordings, and films made based on this principle over the last few years. I myself was one of the featured stars in the movie Pass It On. Rather than saying "If you keep a positive attitude success will eventually come your way" Pass It On went a bit further to say that you must take some kind of action as well, and it gave you insights from many of today's successful individuals to help you understand how to put The Law of Attraction into use for yourself. The experience of working on that project was to coin a phrase "worth a million bucks". I had the great pleasure of working with the most diverse group of folks I could imagine. The knowledge and insight I gained was immeasurable.

After completing the film, the premier, the parties, and speaking engagements associated with this experience, I felt fantastic. Not only had I done something that I thought was truly helpful to others, but I had been a part of something that people might watch and use long after I am gone!

In traveling around speaking I enjoyed helping people to focus on having a positive attitude and using that positive attitude to aid them in achieving their goals. All the while feeling like something was missing. Not knowing or being able to realize what the missing point was it became frustrating to the point that I became my own worst enemy, only partially believing that which I was teaching. This led me to stop speaking and get back to work in my own environment choosing to avoid looking for an answer. This I can tell you was not one of my better decisions. Several months went by without my even thinking about it very much however it was always on my mind in some way or another. Life goes on as we all know and has its ups and downs. I was as happy as I thought I could be, working and enjoying time with family and for us life was truly good. We enjoyed each other's company, more than the vacations, nightlife, cars, houses and other amenities that prosperity and happiness bring. I watched many of my friends continue to work the speaking circuit and occasionally I went and spoke, however, I noticed something had drastically changed within me or with most of the individuals I was speaking with. I had either developed a negative attitude, or they had developed negative practices. Several of my colleagues were becoming so aggressive in making sales and attracting money that I truly felt uncomfortable speaking with them or even being associated with them. Back to my peaceful home environment I retreated. After all if I did not fully believe what I was doing and everyone else was more intent on selling something to the audience rather than actually helping them. I did not want any part of it because some of the things I had heard and seen, in my mind were absolutely atrocious! Although "The Law of Attraction" had become a household word and had developed quite a viral following I soon realized there were flaws in the concept that no one was questioning!

Why question it when people are making millions of dollars through books, CDs, DVDs, seminars, webinars etc? Well the answer to that for me was quite simple! If you are truly concerned with helping people to grow both spiritually and financially you will therefore attract spiritual and financial growth for yourself, but if you preach the Law of Attraction and in truth you are merely seeking people to give you money you will therefore attract people seeking to acquire money as well! By that same token you have just gone to a seminar on the Law of Attraction and rather than focus on spiritual growth ninety percent of you are there to learn how to use the Law of

Attraction for financial gain. By doing this you have attracted someone, (the speaker) whose sole intent is to have you provide financial gain for him! That is how the Law of Attraction is said to work! Think about that and it becomes quite clear. I must admit that we all must make a living and put food on the table that is a given. If we are to believe in something like The Law of Attraction should we not first learn to walk before we run? And before we run should we learn how to first run correctly?

The Law of Attraction teaches us that before we gain success we must develop a positive attitude. I agree with this however is that positive attitude as such: I will concentrate and use all the tools I have learned and have a positive attitude that I will become rich. You will attract lots of people who have that very same attitude they want to be around you because they positively know by doing so they will become rich. The Law of Attraction may be a good concept however most of us jump right in without fully understanding the principle. We have been misled by the modern day snake oil salesman! With the widespread use of email most of us have at one time or another received one of those Nigerian scam emails. "I am Barrister Nigel Foolhardy and I am the administrator of an account that has left you twenty million dollars cash all you have to do is provide me your information and pay the $250.00 filing fee and I will transfer the twenty million to your account!" We delete these emails and laugh yet we attend seminars and hear. "Look at me and how successful and wealthy I am. If you pay $5000.00 for my Law of Attraction training program you will be wealthy and successful as well." Wake up folks! How many times have you seen Bill Gates or Warren Buffet speak and offer to sell you a training package to make you just as wealthy!

The concept of The Law of Attraction could very well work if used properly, however, we must first learn and understand the steps that need to be learned and taken before you jump. A positive attitude is definitely, a requirement however we must also understand what that attitude should be. This book and system will attempt to take an alternative look at the Law of Attraction and provide you the reader with a better understanding of the system of applying the Law of Attraction. We are sure that when you are through learning this system and apply the principals correctly you will agree that it is not enough to have a positive attitude; you must develop a Quantum Attitude!

By understanding the true principals of the Law of Attraction, a positive attitude, and implementing the Quantum Attitude System the Law of Attraction will work for you!

The Quantum Attitude System has been the formula that I have used in filming the movie and creating the numerous books, CDs, DVDs and training courses associated with Quantum Attitude. The following pages will give you a brief idea of Quantum Attitude. The book was inspired by the Quantum Attitude System and in turn this book inspired the film Quantum Attitude.

Glenn Blake

PLANNING

Why is it that most people don't get what they want out of life? I'm not talking about what they think they deserve, but what they truly want. I see so many people trying to win in this "game of life" without a plan. Have you ever seen a football team run onto the field, and play the entire game with no strategy or plan? Most likely not, so why not have a game winning plan in life as well? For the most part, none of us grew up being told that we need a financial plan, other than go to college and get a good job. The world tells us "You need to wake up, go to work, pay bills, and repeat." I think to myself, why should I spend so much time and money on an education, to be making someone else rich? It might be because no one has shown us the proper way to start and own our own business. This book should help you realize that it is not as difficult a task to undertake.

This reference is an easy to understand guide to help people realize that it is not just an idea that gets people to where they want to be, but how to develop that idea into a plan and implement it. We all have planned events in our lives such as birthday parties, weddings, and other social gatherings, but we neglect one of the most important parts in our lives, our own financial well being.

On average, people don't start becoming aware or interested in their own financial situation until they are around 55 years old. Why should you wait until retirement age to become financially savvy?

If you were like me, tired of working for a mediocre paycheck, wanting to be your own boss, ready to be in charge of your own finances instead of just scraping by, owning your own business may be right for you. I'm not saying owning your own business is easy, because it can be time consuming and exhausting, but is a gratifying and rewarding experiences, it's just up to you to get it started.

HOW TO PLAN

Understanding the reason of why you need to have a plan is the best place to start, and now that you have some basic knowledge, let us start with the first phase of planning your business. First, I would recommend doing some research of names and trademarks that you might be interested in using. By doing this research it will help you to avoid trademark infringements as well as allowing you to create a name that is unique, and marketable for your business. How to do this is quite simple-- all you have to do is look up your State Corporation Commission. There should be an entity search which allows you to see if what you may want is already in use. If not in use, you may trademark your name at uspto.com (United States Patent and Trademark Office) although this is not necessary. When establishing this part of your business, you should also consult with an attorney to go over which structure would be best, whether it will be a sole proprietorship, partnership, limited liability company, non-profit, or either corporation. Deciding the structure of your business will determine types of paperwork that need to be filed, taxes, and investment liabilities. Your attorney should give you a description of each structure to help you decide which would be best for you depending on which type of business you will be starting.

My next recommendation would be finding someone in the field in which you want to do business, to act as a mentor/counselor. This person has walked the path in which you are about to embark, and may help with struggles that you may encounter. Some resources to help find such a person is as follows; a Small Business Development Center, Score.org, and SBA.gov.

A Small Business Development Center is usually a government or school run facility that assists entrepreneurs in building skills that are needed to start or purchase a business by providing information and counseling. Anyone seeking to be a business owner is eligible to use their services; thus being a great place to start meeting like minded individuals.

SCORE.org and SBA.gov are both websites that are helpful to you in many ways. There is a wide variety of information available on both websites, and you also have the choice of meeting with a counselor to assist with your entrepreneurial development. Just as a Small Business Development Center, obtaining information from these resources is free and confidential. The valuable assistance from these three venues should help you obtain enough knowledge and expertise to help guide the development of your business.

THE BLUEPRINT

As you may have realized, there are many small steps that you must undertake in becoming a well educated business owner. These steps are leading to your vision; however, being educated is not the only aspect that is needed. You must now be able to put all of your hard work and determination onto paper. You should have the knowledge and the confidence needed to set forth your plan, so let's get started.

When setting up your business plan, it must look professional. It needs to be formatted in a way that will cater to the banks, if you are looking for funding.

Creating a coversheet as well as a table of contents will give the essential information about yourself as well as the information that is included in your plan.

There should be a detailed description of every aspect of the proposed business. A few examples being: how are you going to market it to the public, what is the competition that you will be going up against, how many personnel are going to be needed and at what cost?

When writing the financial aspect of your business, support from a Certified Public Accountant (CPA) should be utilized. Many people underestimate the cost of running a business or fail to realize that there may be unexpected expenses, which could ultimately ruin your business. Included in the financial data, there should be a loan application, a breakdown of equipment and supply list at cost, and a balance sheet. A profit and loss statement should be included as well, as this shows expected revenue coming into your business as well as projected expenses. The profit and loss statement should be paid close attention to, as many over estimate income revenue and under estimate expenses. Over and underestimating can create unnecessary headaches and problems within your business, so be sure to go over your numbers with your CPA. There are a few additional supporting documents to include such as tax returns from all partners and yourself for at least the past three years, a copy of proposed lease or purchase agreements for the space that will be used, and copy of all licenses that will be required to run your business. Lastly, include copies of resumes from all partners and letters of intent from vendors who you will be dealing with.

THE CREATION

Up to this point, everything that you have envisioned should have been pieced together into your business plan. All you have to do now is establish what needs to be done to get your business off the ground. This is where all of your preparation is going to pay off.

Talking with your attorneys you should have established a legal structure for your business, and have legal advice on business law in which your business will pertain, including taxes. This means having all federal, state, and local permits/licenses that are required for your business type. Taxes will depend on the structure of your business that an attorney has explained in detail, whether it is sole proprietorship, LLC, partnership, so on and so forth. Depending on your state, taxes will vary, as there are different tax requirements for each state. Be sure to go over these with your attorney and CPA for full understanding, as well as file for your tax identification number.

When it comes to the physical aspect of your business, location is vital. We have all heard the phrase "location, location, location" and it is the key to helping your business thrive. Understanding demographics and markets is important, as you will need a constant flow of traffic to meet your business expectations. Whether you will be renting or leasing a space for your business, you will in no doubt, be dealing with landlords or realtors. It would be advised to have someone with you who knows how to deal with these contracts. It is also important to know what your rights are as well as understanding the rights of your landlord. Knowing the location needed and the price you can afford is a critical, especially to your finances. There needs to be a sufficient amount of revenue being generated into the business to afford rent and other expenses, while still putting money into your pocket or other business ventures.

Next, we will be discussing how to choose equipment and supplies needed to run your business. Whether you're selling a service or product, you are going to need to know what all costs will be. Vendors will be working for your business, so use this to your advantage. This can be cut throat, but understand that this is where your profit margins come into play. You should never have to overpay for something that you don't have to, communicating with your vendors and having a great rapport can be an advantage. With that said you should be on the road to being a successful business

owner and have your doors open for
business.

NURTURING

If you are now on your way to owning your own successful business, don't start thinking that this is the time to relax. Congratulate yourself and your partners on the hard work and time that all have given, but keep in mind that just because business is open or in the process of it, doesn't mean it will stay open. It is lucrative to your business that you are aware of what is going on not only with the business itself, but the people working to keep it flourishing.

The initial stage of business is exciting, but there are many moving variables that will need to be dealt with. All employees and partners must understand what their roles are and figure out how to meet these goals that are set. In order to do this, some people find that having group meetings bring each other to the point of understanding from sharing different view points, all the while showing leadership skills from everyone involved.

Staying focused on your goal and using every available resource from starting your business to keeping it open will allow for a profitable growth for you and everyone involved. By incorporating all valuable resources you should be well on your way to forming and running a successful business.

The Quantum Attitude System has been designed using common sense and proven facts. The Quantum Attitude System should be referenced whenever you have questions regarding your business plan. For more information, literature, and DVD's on applying the Quantum Attitude System please visit us at www.quantum-attitude.com

ABOUT THE AUTHOR

Cyle Grieve grew up in New Mexico and now resides in Arizona with his family. Where he is now actively pursuing his entrepreneurial endeavors and is presently writing and speaking on the application of the Quantum Attitude System principles.

www.ingramcontent.com/pod-product-compliance
Lightning Source LLC
Chambersburg PA
CBHW051302170526
45165CB00004B/1820